FEMALE
SPORTS STARS

CHELSEA HOUSE PUBLISHERS

FEMALE SPORTS
STARS

SUPERSTARS
OF WOMEN'S
TRACK AND FIELD

Martha Wickham

CHELSEA HOUSE PUBLISHERS
Philadelphia

CHELSEA HOUSE PUBLISHERS

Produced by Daniel Bial Agency and Associates
New York, New York

Senior Designer   Cambraia Magalhães
Picture Research   Sandy Jones
Cover Illustration   Bonnie Gardner
Frontispiece photo   Florence Griffith-Joyner

First Printing
1 3 5 7 9 8 6 4 2

Library of Congress Cataloging-in-Publication Data

Wickham, Martha, 1963–
    Superstars of women's track and field / Martha Wickham.
      p.   cm. — (Female sports stars)
    Includes bibliographical references (p.) and index.
Summary: Traces the achievements of some of the top women track and field athletes,
including Wilma Rudolph, Grete Waitz, Joan Benoit Samuelson, Florence Griffith Joyner,
and Jackie Joyner-Kersee.
ISBN 0-7910-4394-0 (hardcover)
1. Women track and field athletes—Biography—Juvenile literature. [1. Track and field
athletes. 2. Women—Biography.] I. Title.
II. Series.
GV697.A1W538   1996
796.42'092'2—dc20
[B]   96-32154
                                                                                                      CIP
                                                                                                       AC

CONTENTS

GO FOR THE GOLD

Female athletes have never had things easy, as you will see from the stories in this book. To be a world-class athlete always means making difficult choices and working hard to achieve one's goals. Nowadays, athletics is an open field for many women. The only thing keeping an athlete back is the limitations of her body and her ability to dream. But that was not always the case.

For example, it took many years for women's achievements to be measured at the Olympics. No women were allowed to participate in the first of the modern Olympics, which was held in Athens, Greece, in 1896. In the 1900 games held in Paris, France, women were allowed to compete only in golf and tennis. At the next Games, in 1904, women were again officially barred from Olympic competition. (Several women entered an unofficial archery contest, and Lida Howell of the United States won three gold medals.)

In 1908, women were back in the Games but were only allowed to compete in figure skating, archery, and tennis. At the 1912 Games, they were restricted to swimming competitions. Women's sports got a bit of a boost in 1923. In that year, Lou Henry Hoover (whose husband, Herbert, later became a U.S. president), organized the Women's Division of the National Amateur Athletic Federation. The motto chosen was "A sport for every girl and every girl in a sport."

By the 1928 Games, regulations had loosened up enough to allow women in certain track-and-field events: the 100-meter dash, the 800-meter run, the 400-meter relay, the running high jump, and the discus throw. In 1932, women's track and field had its first big star, Babe Didrikson, who won two gold medals. Nowadays, the Olympics features women competing in 19 events, including long road races, hurdles, and the heptathlon (a competition that demands its adherents to be excel at seven different track-and-field events). In addition, women compete in dozens of other sports at the Summer and Winter Olympics.

It also took many years before women athletes were able to make a living at their sport. Grete Waitz, for instance, was one of the first to realize she could earn a living from running the marathon. She quit her teaching job; sometimes when she went for a training run, she left a note saying, "I've gone to work. Be back in an hour." However, it was not until 1976, after she had made two Olympic teams, that she received her first free pair of sneakers from a sponsor!

Today, a number of female track-and-field stars—such as Joan Benoit Samuelson, Florence Griffith Joyner, and Jackie Joyner-Kersee—are highly sought for endorsements and speaking engagements. But they did not reach the top of their sport because they were seeking financial success. Indeed, they have been motivated by the same thing that pushed Lida Howell in 1904: the desire to be the very best at what they do.

1

WILMA RUDOLPH: THE WORLD'S FASTEST WOMAN

Wilma Rudolph was born on June 23, 1940, in the small town of St. Bethlehem, Tennessee. She was the twentieth of 22 children. Her father worked as a porter, and her mother did housework for several families in their town. When Wilma was very young, the family moved to Clarksville, Tennessee.

Wilma was born almost two months premature, and weighed only four and a half pounds at birth. Perhaps because of these circumstances, Wilma was plagued by almost constant illness as a young girl. Clarksville had only one black doctor, but Mrs. Rudolph was adept at creating special "home remedies" for her sickly daughter. When Wilma was four, she came close to dying from double pneumonia which was fol-

Wilma Rudolph flies out of the starting blocks at the 1960 Olympics.

lowed by scarlet fever. When she finally recovered, her family discovered that there was something wrong with her left leg. During her last illness, Wilma had contracted polio.

The polio had damaged her left leg. The weakened leg simply couldn't hold Wilma up. Doctors in Clarksville didn't think she would ever walk again. But Mrs. Rudolph did not give up easily. Determined to find special doctors for her daughter, she brought Wilma by bus to Nashville. Even in Nashville the doctors were not encouraging.

The doctors recommended Mrs. Rudolph bring Wilma to the hospital in Nashville every day for the massage therapy. However, the hospital was 40 miles from the Rudolph's home. Mrs. Rudolph could not afford the time off from work or the bus fare for the daily commute. So she asked the doctors to teach her how to do the massage. Everyday, Mrs. Rudolph massaged Wilma's leg, and once a week she made the hospital run to Nashville with her young daughter.

After two years of the treatments, the doctors noticed very little improvement and tried to get Mrs. Rudolph to accept Wilma's condition. She refused to give up on her daughter though. The whole family rallied to Wilma's cause and took turns giving massages.

When Wilma was six, she was finally able to get around on her own. She enrolled at Cobb Elementary School. Wilma was delighted to be in school, although sometimes the other children teased her and made fun of her awkward gait. Their teasing just made Wilma determined to get better. The doctors made a brace for her leg, and this helped her, too. When the brace was no longer useful, they made a high-topped shoe. Soon Wilma was able to go anywhere she wanted. One day Mrs. Rudolph she came

home from work to find Wilma, barefoot, running around their yard. Wilma was better!

Wilma had watched countless hours of pick-up basketball games in her neighborhood. She'd studied players and plays and had learned what would work and what wouldn't on the basketball court When she started high school, she made up her mind to be a varsity basketball player. She practiced and drilled, and at fifteen, she was named an all-state basketball player. When Ed Temple, the women's track coach at Tennessee A and I University, saw her on the basketball court, he knew that he wanted her on his track team. Temple refereed at a high school championship game at which Wilma played. When he saw the tall, graceful girl with the long, long legs, Temple recognized a sprinter in the making. He offered her a full, four-year athletic scholarship.

Wilma had never been so far from home before. She found the training schedule very difficult and missed her big family. One day she told Ed Temple that she wanted to go home. He

In 1956, few people expected much of the 16-year-old Wilma Rudolph when she showed up at the Olympics trials. But here she runs stride for stride with Mae Faggs (right) and wins a spot on the U.S. Women's Olympic track team.

allowed her to go, but told her not to come back unless she would stick with his program.

Wilma went home. She was delighted to be with her parents, but she soon realized that she did not want to lose what might be her only opportunity to develop her talents. Soon she was starring for her college track team and attracting attention with her blazing speed.

For a young black girl from a small southern town, the Olympics seemed impossibly far off. This was especially true in 1956, when the Games were held in Melbourne, Australia. But Wilma, only 16 years old, decided to go to Seattle, Washington, for the Olympic tryouts. She qualified for the 200-meter dash by tying for first place in her heat. The woman she crossed the finish line with was Mae Faggs, a U.S. record holder and two-time Olympian. Faggs took Wilma under her wing. She encouraged the youngster to stop worrying about trying to fit in and not make others feel badly when she won.

On the third day of the Melbourne Games, Wilma ran her first Olympic race. It was a qualifying race for the 200-meter dash. Although she was extremely nervous, she managed to finish in third place. The next day the semifinal race was held. Again, Wilma finished third. Unfortunately, only the first two finishers of this race advanced to the final race. Wilma had been eliminated.

Three days later, however, she returned to the Olympic Stadium to compete in the 400-meter relay with three teammates: Mae Faggs, Margaret Matthews, and Isabelle Daniels. When the starter's gun went off, Faggs ran a very strong first leg, leaving the Americans tied for first place. Matthews lost ground in her second leg before handing off to Wilma. Wilma ran an excellent leg, bringing her team into third place. She handed off to Daniels, who was able to hold their position. The heavily favored Soviet and German teams won the gold and silver medals; the American women captured third place and the bronze medal.

After the Melbourne Olympics, Wilma became determined to win a gold medal at the next Games, to be held in Rome. She returned to Tennessee and trained harder than ever. However, she fell in love with a fellow student named Robert Eldridge, and soon she was pregnant. Wilma left school for one year and had a baby girl. When the new school year started, Wilma was back training on the track at Tennessee State.

At the beginning of her sophomore year, Wilma began to lose races to her teammates. Wilma and Coach Temple were extremely concerned because this was the year of the trials for the 1960 Olympic Games. Coach Temple could find nothing wrong with her style and technique. Finally, a team doctor diagnosed a recurring tonsil infection. Wilma had a tonsillectomy, recovered, and found herself racing better than ever.

In August 1960, at the Olympic trials, Wilma sparkled during the 100- and 200-meter dashes. She was delighted to learn, also, that three of her Tennessee State teammates would join her, forming a practiced, mature team for the 400-meter relay race. Wilma was even happier to learn that her beloved Coach Temple had been named coach of the U.S. Olympic women's track team.

The U.S. team arrived in Rome early for the games, giving the athletes a chance to get used to the hot Italian summer. For Wilma and her teammates, accustomed to running in the Tennessee heat, the weather posed no problem. On the Tuesday before the Games began, though, disaster struck. As Wilma jogged across a field, she stepped in a small hole and felt her ankle pop. The team doctor could not guarantee that her ankle would be healed before the competition began. He ordered her to rest for a few days.

The ankle responded to the rest, and Wilma easily won the first heat of the 100-meter dash. In the second heat, she tied the world record of 11.3 seconds. When the gun went off for the finals, it looked as though Maria Itkina of the USSR was going to win. Wilma held on, though, and soon had a healthy lead which she turned into an easy win. She completed the race in a world-record pace of 11.0 seconds. The world-record did not hold, however, because the wind was clocked at 2.752 meters per second, at Wilma's back. Since the accepted standard was 2.0 seconds, her record was disqualified. Still, Wilma had her first gold medal!

Next came the 200-meter dash. This time, Wilma set an Olympic record of 23.2 seconds in her first heat. In the finals, her time of 24.0 seconds was not a record, but it was enough to win Wilma another gold medal! Again, Wilma defeated an extremely strong opponent, Jutta Heine of Germany.

Wilma was elated with her victories, but she worried about her ankle. It had held up during her sprints, but both previous races had been run on the straight section of the track. Would her ankle hold during the relay race

Wilma Rudolph breaks the tape of the women's 400-meter relay race to win her third gold medal at the 1960 Olympics.

which would require her to run around the curving part of the track?

The first three legs of the relay ran without a problem. When it came down to Wilma's dash, however, there was a problem. The baton hand-off was botched! Wilma had to come to a complete stop to receive the baton, and during this time the Russians were able to move into the lead. Wilma set off blazing. With every step she reduced the yardage between her and the Soviet speedster. At the last second, Wilma surged across the finish line, beating the Russian runner by just three-tenths of a second. Wilma had her third gold medal of the games!

The American media dubbed Wilma Rudolph "the Black Gazelle." Fans adored her, and Wilma was always gracious and kind to them. When she got back to America, President Kennedy invited her to the White House. Although 1960 was the year that blacks were elected to Congress for the first time (three members sat that year), and the Ku Klux Klan still marched against Civil Rights, Wilma was a national hero. She was named Sportsman of the Year by European sportswriters and was voted Woman Athlete of the Year in the United States.

After the Games, she married Robert and finished her degree. She wrote an autobiography, and served as a Goodwill Ambassador the United States to French West Africa. She was inducted into the Black Athletes Hall of Fame and taught at UCLA.

Wilma died in 1994, but her achievements remain among the most impressive of any athlete. The girl from a poor family whom many doctors had said would never walk ended up the fastest female runner in the world—and an inspiration for all people.

2

GRETE WAITZ: WORLD-CLASS ATHLETE

Grete Anderson Waitz was born in November 1953 and was raised near Oslo, Norway. An active child, she used to pit herself against a bus or a car and try to outrun it. If she was given chores to do, she would test herself to see how quickly she could complete them, running to and from the grocery store, for instance. When she would play cops and robbers with neighborhood children, no one wanted to be the cop when she was the robber—because they could never catch her!

Grete was born the only girl and youngest child in a middle-class family. Her brothers, Jan and Arild, were nine and three respectively when Grete was born. Her parents were delighted to have a little girl at last and dressed her in pretty dresses every Sunday for church. They also insisted that she take piano lessons. Grete was not interested in dresses or the piano.

Grete Waitz winning the 1983 New York City Marathon.

When she was twelve years old, she took her first training run. She laced up an old pair of running spikes that she found lying around and ran back and forth on a patch of grass behind her house. This was to become her first regular training regimen. A few months later, when she found that she still enjoyed running, she decided that she needed to join a sports club. The schools she attended had no organized running program. Her brother Jan already belonged to a track and field club in Oslo but it allowed no girls. A neighbor belonged to the Vidar Sports Club which did admit girls and Jan helped get her accepted there. With another friend for company, Grete packed a gym bag and walked twenty minutes to the club, as they didn't have money for a bus. Grete still belongs to the Vidar Sports Club to this day.

A year later, when she was thirteen, Grete won her first prize for a track and field event. It was for a type of ball-throwing event that is unique to Norway. However, she finished near the back of the pack in all the 60-meter and 100-meter sprint races she ran. When she entered a 300-meter cross-country race, though, she performed better. She did not win the race, but her time was fast enough for her to be noticed.

At this point, Grete began running with the older boys at the club. These young men allowed her to join them on their longer runs, usually about six miles. It was difficult for her, but she managed to keep up with their fast and grueling 6:30-per-mile pace. She began to realize that her real strength was distance running, not sprinting.

When she was 14, Grete won her first race, a 400-meter cross-country event. At 16, she became the Norwegian Junior Champion in the 400 and 800 meters. She also made her first senior national team that year, and traveled to Canada to compete. It was her very first trip outside of Scandinavia. She did not win in Canada but being chosen for the team made her realize that she could become an athlete to reckon with if she devoted herself.

For Grete, this was not a problem. She gave up the piano and other outside activities and concentrated on running and her schoolwork. These two passions came together when she had to write a paper for school on the "Person I Most Admire." She chose to write about Wilma Rudolph.

At 17, she competed in the European Championships in Helsinki, Finland. In the summer of that year, 1971, she set Norwegian records for the 800 and 1,500 meters. When she reached the European Championships, however, the pressure she felt too much to handle. She ran two disappointing races and was upset, hurt, and extremely disillusioned with international athletics. Rather than let her emotions get the best of her, Grete vowed to fight on. She determined to go to Rome in 1974, the sight of the next European Championships, and prove herself. "I'm going to do well there," she said to herself. "I'm going to show these people."

At this point, Grete faced a crisis in her personal life. Her boyfriend, who was also her coach, was diagnosed with cancer. She watched him grow thinner and sicker, but refused to admit he would not get well again. When he died, Grete was in shock. She lost her desire to do anything, even to eat. She was not running and she was not socializing. When friends from the Vidar Sports Club saw how devastated she was, they began to take her out to eat, to dance, to run, and to have fun. Gradually, Grete began to resume her training schedule. She used the running as a way to deal with her grief. Among the group of runners who helped pull Grete out of her slump was a young man named Jack Waitz. Grete fell in love with him.

The 1972 Olympics, held in Munich, were a turning point for Grete. She ran a personal best of 4:16 in the 1,500 meters. This did not win her a medal, but it did wonders for her poise and self-confidence. That same year she began a winning streak in Norway that was to last for 12 years. She was named Athlete of the Year in Norway in 1975, after she won a bronze medal in the 1,500 meters in the 1974 European Championships in Rome.

Also in 1975, Grete and Jack were married. The morning of their wedding they got lost on a long run, and almost didn't make it to the church in time. The following morning, they were back on the track, doing difficult training work!

Grete was ranked number one in the world in 1975 for the 1,500 and 3,000 meters and set her first world record in the 3,000 race. She did not medal at the 1976 Olympics, despite setting a Scandinavian record for the 1,500-meter run. She returned to Norway from the Olympics tired and dispirited. She felt she had run the race of her life, and it had not been enough to win. Realizing that she was exhausted from overtraining and maintaining an extremely hectic schedule, she cut back on her running and competed in cross-country skiing and team handball. She rested, enjoyed her running, and regained her confidence. The respite paid off, and her times that year were personal bests. At the first World Cup, in 1977, she won the gold medal in the 3,000-meter race.

After the 1978 European Championships, in Prague, where she won only a bronze medal, Grete considered retirement. She'd had a relatively long and successful track career. She had done some traveling, had some new experiences, and could have given it up to pursue her teaching career and a family with Jack.

Jack had other ideas. He'd been reading lots of running magazines and he thought Grete's next move should be to a longer race—the marathon. What's more, Jack thought she should tackle the 1978 New York City Marathon. Grete thought he was crazy; after all, she'd never run more than 12 miles at a time before.

To celebrate its 25th anniversary, the New York City Marathon put laurels on the heads of its greatest winners. Bill Rodgers (left) won four times between 1976 and 1979. Alberto Salazar (right) won three times between 1980 and 1982. Grete Waitz (center) won nine times between 1978 and 1988.

Jack's hunch about Grete's abilities proved correct. She not only won the New York City Marathon, she set a world record in the process! Grete found her life changing. Used to living quietly with Jack in Norway, she began receiving invitations to races and running clinics all over the world. She was amazed by all the attention, and happy to help out at clinics and help popularize the sport she loved, but she began to feel torn. She enjoyed helping people and racing around the world, but she needed time to concentrate on her training and racing.

Grete went back to New York City to run the marathon in 1979, and turned in another world record performance: 2:27:33. No woman had ever run a marathon in under two-and-a-half hours. Not only had Grete done that, she lopped nearly another two-and-a-half minutes off that time as well!

Grete won the New York City marathon again in 1980 with another record of 2:25:42. Injury forced her to drop out of the 1981 race, but she was back, victorious, in 1983. In 1983 she also won the London Marathon, with a world record time of 2:25:29. In addition, 1983 also found her winning a gold medal at the IAAF World Championships, with a 2:28:09 marathon. In 1984 she raced against Joan Benoit Samuelson and a field of other talented runners in the Los Angeles Olympic Games. Although Samuelson "expected to see Grete Waitz within range," during miles five and six, Grete couldn't keep up with Joan's blistering pace. Grete finished second to win a silver medal for her 2:26:18 race. She came back to win two more New York City marathons, in 1984 and 1985.

While Grete was winning marathons around the world, she was also winning medals in international cross-country championships. From 1978 to 1981 she was awarded gold medals for those races. She won only a bronze in 1982 and 1984, but she won another gold in 1983.

She is a six-time winner of the L'eggs Mini Marathon, and has received awards from *Runner's World* magazine, which awarded her its Paavo Nurmi Award; *People* magazine, which named her one of 1980's "Notable Personalities of the Year"; and the King of Norway's St. Olav's Medal. She was elected to the executive board of the Norwegian Olympic Committee in 1985.

Although no longer racing at the world-class level, Grete continues to run and attend clinics. She maintains her simple life style in her beloved Norway, and remains an inspiration to runners everywhere.

3

JOAN BENOIT SAMUELSON: MAINE'S HERO

Joan Benoit was born in 1957 and raised in Cape Elizabeth, Maine. Her parents were both long-time Maine residents. Her father's family had founded Benoit's, a retail clothing business in the state. Her mother was a transplant from Massachusetts, where her father had been the city editor at the old Boston Herald. Joan inherited her sense of adventure and daring from both parents. As a young man, her father spent much of World War II in the Tenth Mountain Division, which was the ski troops. Her mother joined the American Red Cross and spent the war in India and China. The two adventurers were introduced by a mutual friend at a party back in Cape Elizabeth, fell in love, and were married after the war.

Joan Benoit carries the American flag on her victory lap after the marathon at the 1984 Olympics.

Their children, Andre Jr., Peter, Joan, and John were introduced to skiing early in life. A special pair of skis was stored in the basement and dragged out as soon as a Benoit child was considered old enough to learn. By the time Joan was ready, the skis were battered and scratched. She didn't care. One Saturday, when she was about three, her parents and older brothers went off skiing. Joan found the "official first pair of skis" in the basement. Soon, she was schussing down their steep front lawn—falling often. Her parents didn't relent that year, but the following season she was allowed to join the family at Sugarloaf Mountain for the first time.

Joan was not especially interested in running as a child. She was an athletic little girl and ran and jumped and played with her brothers and other children, but her main interest was skiing. She decided while still young that she wanted to be a championship skier. She did everything she could to ski; in her teens, she worked at a ski lodge so that she could be close to the action.

Although she was a superb athlete, her experience was not all positive. In the very beginning, she fell often and was cold and damp much of the day. She also had trouble with the T-bar, which is one type of ski lift that carries skiers to the top of the mountain. She was too small to ride the lift properly, so she had to hang on, as she notes, "like a monkey" all the way to the top. She never gave up; her love for skiing made her keep at the T-bar until she had mastered it. She credits these early skiing experiences with giving her the ability to cope with discomfort and the drive to be her best—qualities which helped tremendously when she turned her attention to distance running.

In September 1973, Joan had been skiing all day. Although it was starting to get dark out, she insisted on trying a slalom run one more time, pushing to increase her speed. In the middle of the course she lost her concentration and crashed into one of the gates. She heard her leg break; she cried, but more out of surprise and frustration than pain. She was carried down the mountain on the ski patrol toboggan, and cared for at the Maine Medical Center in Portland.

Joan worried about being away from skiing, and also from the track. She had started running for the girl's track team during her freshman year at Cape Elizabeth High School. That spring, when her cast finally came off, she hung around the track field, wishing she could join in. She volunteered to rake the long-jump pit during practice just to be around the team. A couple of weeks after the cast was removed she decided to try a run. An incident occurred then which she still remembers today. She'd been running for some time when a little boy, crossing a field nearby, stopped to watch her. When she stopped to rest, he came up to her, shook his head, and said, "You shouldn't run when you're limping." She recognized this as good advice but she just had to keep on running.

Joan continued to run that year and developed an intense love of the sport. The next ski season, when she returned to the top of the mountain, she was surprised to find herself nervous and scared. This time, Joan listened to her mind and body. She knew that she could not be a world-class racer if she was afraid of the mountain. Still, she could continue to dream about winning an Olympic gold medal— even if it came from running, not skiing.

Joan's real running career began when she was eight years old, at a gymkana in Norfolk, Connecticut. The gymkana is basically a track and field event for children. The Benoits had cousins who lived in Norfolk, so Joan and her older brother Peter were invited down for the competition, which is really just a chance for children to have some fun and run around. One of the first events of the day was the 880-yard dash for teenage boys. Joan watched the winner with fascination. While she was trying to figure out what had enabled the boy run so fast, she overheard a woman behind her say, "You can tell Jim runs for the high school team. Look at the way he carries his arms." Joan noted that he kept his arms close to his sides and ran with his elbows tucked in to his waist. His head and upper body hardly moved—he used all his energy on his legs.

Little Joan thought this was good advice, and she used it that day and all through her running career. She had signed up for five running and two jumping events. Using Jim's running style, she went home with five blue first-place ribbons!

When she got to Cape Elizabeth High School, Joan added field hockey, a fall sport, to her roster. Although she wasn't a "natural" hockey player, she practiced extra hours and showed her coaches that she was a dedicated and thoughtful player. Even during the field hockey season, with its intense days of training, Joan managed to fit an evening run into her schedule. Her training paid off; she was named the team's Most Valuable Player during her junior year. In addition, she was named the track team's Most Valuable Player during her freshman year.

During the fall of her sophomore year, Joan's running career took another turn.

Although she had always concentrated on the longest races available, these were always relatively short. The longest race available to her was the mile. One day in 1972, Joan was putting on her cleats for hockey practice when one of the boys from the cross-country team (there were no girl's cross-country teams at that time) mentioned that their opponent was bringing a girl along—a girl who competed with the boys. Joan's classmate wanted to know if she wanted to test herself against the opposing girl. Joan was already running longer distances in private practices. She got permission from her hockey coach, called her Mom to bring her running shoes to school, and entered the race. Joan easily beat the girl over a course 2.5 miles long. She felt terrific, and went back to hockey practice at the end of the race.

Benoit had time to wave to the crowd as she finished the first women's marathon in Olympic history.

The following summer, after her skiing accident, Joan joined Country Runners, a club in Buckfield, Maine, coached by Ron Thompson. She was able to participate in cross-country races all over the state during that summer and the following year. She took first place in her age group at the Amateur Athletic Union women's cross-country meet in Scarborough, Maine, that year. Then she went on to the regionals in Amherst, Massachusetts, where she placed 17th out of a field of 70 runners. She entered the Great Pumpkin Classic, held in South Hiram, Maine, that fall. Out of a field of 57 runners, Joan came in first. The following spring, she set a course record at the Maine Masters 5 kilometer (3.1 miles) road race in Portland.

That summer, Joan continued running in AAU-sponsored road races around New England. At a competition in Boston, she met John Babington, the coach of the Liberty Athletic Club. In the fall of 1974, John invited Joan to join his club. Being a member of the Liberty A.C. would give Joan wider exposure and more intense competition.

She won the Great Pumpkin Classic again during her senior year. Then she ran in the National Road Runners Age Group Competition in Van Cortlandt Park in New York City and finished ninth in a field of 75 runners. At the AAU finals in Gorham, Maine, she ran 15:30 for 2.3 miles. She also scored 13 goals for the field hockey team that season. That fall she also qualified for the National Junior Olympics Cross-Country Championships in Raleigh, North Carolina. She ran a respectable race in the Championships, but far enough back in the teens to make her realize that, if she was really serious about running, she'd have to make a total commitment.

The spring of her senior year, Joan decided the train with the boys' track team at Cape Elizabeth High. This way she could receive better coaching and face stiffer competition. She began to run double workouts: she would take a run in the morning then go to track practice in the afternoon. At the State Triple C Division Championships she was first in the 880 with a time of 2:22.2, first in the 440 at 1:02.4, second in the long jump, and fifth in the 220. At the regional meet in Westbrook, Maine, she ran the mile in 5:15, an unofficial record. At the State Finals, she ran the mile in 5:29, breaking the state record.

In the August before going off to college, she ran in the Junior Olympic Trials. The Trials were held at Cornell University, in Ithaca, New York. Joan ran the mile in 5:01.1. It was not a winning time, but it was 2 seconds better than her fastest time.

Joan had chosen to attend Bowdoin College, her father's alma mater, even though it did not field a women's running team. At Bowdoin, she played field hockey, fitting her runs in before and after hockey practices. She also continued to travel and run road races with the Liberty Athletic Club. During a hockey game near the end of the season, Joan stepped into a divot and twisted her knee. The college physician, Dan Hanley, treated her injury. A friend of his, who knew a lot about running, had seen Joan run at the Olympic Trials in Oregon the previous summer. The friend had asked Dr. Hanley why Joan wasn't devoting herself strictly to running. Dr. Hanley posed the question to Joan during the examination: Why would she risk injury playing a lateral-motion sport like field hockey when her talent was for running?

This was all the encouragement that Joan needed. She had been thinking about giving up field hockey to concentrate on running. The idea was scary for her, though, because she would be leaving the comfortable world of college-sponsored sport for one where she'd need to find her own coaches, her own races, and develop her own strategies. Still, Joan felt she was ready.

In April of her sophomore year, Joan went to Philadelphia for the prestigious Penn Relays. She placed fourth in the 1,500-meter run with a time of 4:28.27. With the 1980 Olympics coming up, she was trying to make the event her specialty. The next month she ran her first L'eggs Mini Marathon in New York City. In June she went to the Junior and Senior AAU National meets at the University of California at Los Angeles and placed seventh in the 3,000-meter run.

That fall, her junior year, Joan transferred to North Carolina State University with an athletic scholarship. She had loved Bowdoin, but she felt she needed a strong women's running program and North Carolina State had one. Also, the athletic scholarship would help her family's finances tremendously.

Almost from the start, Joan realized that the transfer was a mistake. She wasn't nearly as happy at North Carolina State. She raced with the women's team and continued to improve her times but felt lost at the large school. During the spring semester, Joan became ill with mononucleosis and missed the rest of the regulation track season. That summer, recovering from the illness, she ran the 1980 Olympic Trials, held in Eugene, Oregon in the 1,500-meter run but failed to qualify for the team.

She returned to NC State for one more semester, at the urging of the Coach Russ

Combs. She set a world best at the Bonne Bell 10K (6.2 miles) on October 9. When she returned to Bowdoin for the second semester of her junior year, she found that the college had finally organized a women's running team. That January she traveled to Bermuda to run in Bermuda 10K. Feeling strong and confident, she won that race. The following day was the marathon. During a training run that morning, her training partner suggested that they enter the marathon. More on a whim than anything else, Joan agreed. Although her heel was sore from the 10K, and she had never run a marathon (26.3 miles) before, Joan finished second. Her time of 2:50.54 was fast enough to qualify her for the Boston Marathon in April.

Before she could get to Boston, the oldest regularly-run marathon in the country, Joan had to recover from the damage she had   done to her heel in running the impromptu marathon in Bermuda. She rested for a few weeks, then slowly resumed her training. She ran, "about a hundred miles the week before the Boston race," and knew she was in great shape. Still, the marathon is a grueling race. A runner needs to be prepared intellectually and emotionally to deal with the rigors of running such a long race.

On April 16, 1979, Joan won the Boston Marathon. Not only had she beaten the heavily-favored Patti Lyons, her time of 2:35.15 was a new American and course record for women. She received a congratulatory phone call from

President Bill Clinton, who likes to jog, has good company on this 1995 outing. To the right is Bill Rodgers, who won the Boston Marathon four times, and center is Joan Benoit Samuelson, whose first major victory also came at the Boston Marathon.

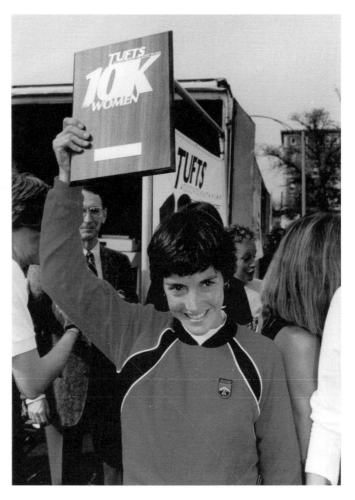

*Joan continued winning
after the Olympics. Here
she is all smiles after
winning the 1985 Tufts
10 kilometer road race
in Boston.*

President Jimmy Carter who invited her to the
White House for dinner.

Because of her three semesters at North
Caroline State, Joan was behind on the credits
necessary to graduate from Bowdoin. She
spent one extra semester at the school, in the
fall of 1979. After graduation, Joan spent some
time in New Zealand training with elite runners
there.

Joan set her sights on the 1984 Olympics.
In 1980, she broke Patti Lyon's record in the
Litchfield Road Race, then came in fourth in the
Cascade Runoff in Oregon. In 1981 she won

the Anheuser-Busch Natural Light Half-Marathon in New Orleans with an American best of 1:13.26 and again in San Diego with another record of 1:11.16. She finished third in the Boston Marathon that year.

The heel injury she'd sustained in Bermuda came back to bother her. At the TAC National 10,000 finals in Sacramento, California, Joan ran a winning 33:37.5. That evening her heels began to hurt more than ever. For the next couple of weeks she swam and rode a bike instead of running to remove some of the pressure from her feet. By July, she was back to running more than ten miles a day again, even though her heels continued to hurt. In August, she ran the Avon International Marathon in Ottawa, Canada, in 2:37.24. Later that fall she had surgery to correct the heel problem.

By May she was back to her top running form. She ran the Old Kent River Bank Run, a 25K (15.5 miles) with a winning time of 1:26.30, taking 10 seconds off her own American record time. On Memorial Day, she finished second in the L'eggs Mini Marathon, behind Grete Waitz. She ran a personal best of 32:35. She ran a 10K in Middletown, New York on July 18, winning in 33:17. In early September she ran the Nike/Oregon Track Club Marathon in 2:26:11, a new American record and her first sub-2:30 marathon.

Her strategy for 1983, with the Olympics a year away, was to keep running races of different lengths. The International Olympic Committee had announced the inclusion of the marathon for women at the 1984 Games (the first time ever). Joan not only wanted to run the marathon there, she also hoped to qualify for the 3,000 meters. She won the 3,000M at a TAC meet in Boston in January and the mile at a Boston Track Club meet a month later, running her best time, 4:36.48. In April, she ran the Boston Marathon with a world record time of 2:22:43. She also came in first in the Philadelphia Distance Run in September, running the 13.1 mile course in 1:09:16 and setting a new American record. In December of 1983, Joan's college boyfriend, Scott Samuelson proposed. Now Joan had the Olympics and a wedding to plan for.

Back in Maine to train for the Olympic Marathon trials, she started to feel pain in her knee. Soon the pain became another sensation, and her knee began to lock. Joan tried to rest the joint and would have some good training days, then her knee would lock up again and she'd be unable to run. Finally, in April 1984, with the Trials looming close ahead of her, Joan underwent arthroscopic surgery on her knee. The surgeons found a fibrous mass called a plica which had become inflamed and interfered with the knee joint. Joan rested after surgery, but decided, on May 2, that she had to begin training if she had any hope of performing well in the Trials, now just 10 days away. Nervous and unsure of the leg, Joan resumed her training.

At the Trials, held in Olympia, Washington, Joan ran a cautious and conservative race. She took the lead at mile 14 and ran to victory with a time of 2:31:41. She was far from her world record, but her leg had held up and she'd made the U.S. Olympic Women's Marathon team.

On June 17 she ran in the Olympic Trials Exhibition 10,000 meter race, which was held in the Los Angeles Coliseum. She won the event in 32:07. The event had not been approved for the 1984 Olympics, but Joan was delighted with the sign that her leg had fully recovered.

At the Olympics, held in Los Angeles, Joan gathered with the other contenders at Santa Monica College. For the first three miles, she ran with the pack, but then she broke away because she felt hemmed in by the other runners. She kept expecting one of the other racers to catch her, but they never did. Ingrid Kristiansen, who ended up in second place, noted that all the leaders were waiting for experienced marathoner Grete Waitz to make her move. Kristiansen said, "If I'd followed Joanie, maybe three or four other girls would have come too. It might have been a different race." When 16 miles passed, and then 20, she felt strong and in control. The marathon ended in the Los Angeles Coliseum. Joan remembers thinking, as she entered the ramp leading into the Coliseum, that "once you leave this tunnel your life will be changed forever." The crowd roared when she emerged from the tunnel. Her mother later told her that she looked like a little gray mouse skittering out of a hole. She ran her final lap around the track, then broke the tape with a time of 2:24:52, a full minute and a half ahead of the second place finisher. Joan had her Olympic gold!

Joan's accomplishment was amazing especially considering how recently she had had knee surgery. She returned to Portland as a hero. For her accomplishments, Joan has been award the Sullivan Award and the Jesse Owens Award.

4

FLORENCE GRIFFITH JOYNER: "FLO JO"

Florence Griffith Joyner was not always known as "Fluorescent Flo," or as the superstar of the 1988 Olympics in Seoul, South Korea. But she was always a determined and creative child. Born on December 21, 1959, Florence Delorez Griffith was the seventh of 11 children. Her mother, Florence, had left North Carolina for California as a young women, hoping to find a career modeling. When that dream eluded her, she married Robert Griffith, an airline electronics engineer. In 1964, when Florence was five, her mother packed up her children and left the Mojave Desert, where they had been living, and Robert. She resettled in Los Angeles, where she hoped to find a better life.

Mrs. Griffith was a strict disciplinarian. Florence Delorez, known as Dee Dee, was not

Florence Griffith-Joyner wore this hooded outfit during the heats for for the 100-meter race at the 1988 Olympics.

allowed to watch television on weekdays, and bedtime was always 10:00, even during high school. Dee Dee, however, found ways to assert her independence. She kept a diary, developed a love of poetry, and became a very creative hair-stylist. Sometimes other kids used to laugh at her inventive hairstyles, but Dee Dee didn't care.Eventually, other girls asked her to style their hair for them. In high school, Dee Dee decided to get a pet. Rather than settle for something ordinary such as a dog or cat, she bought a boa constrictor!

She also discovered she was good at athletics. When she was seven, Dee Dee entered a Sugar Ray Robinson Youth Foundation competition in Los Angeles. She beat the other children, but was too shy to talk to Sugar Ray at the awards ceremony. Her mother remembers that Dee Dee was so graceful that, even when walking, she looked like a ballerina. When she would visit her father, back in the Mojave Desert, Dee Dee would do unconventional sprints running after jackrabbits.

Dee Dee attended Jordan High School in Los Angeles. Although she set school records in the sprints and the long jump, she could not seem to beat another girl, Valerie Brisco, at a neighboring high school.

When Dee Dee graduated from Jordan High in 1978, she decided to attended California State University. A serious student, she earned good grades while working toward a business degree. She also joined the track team, where she ran the 200-meter and 400-meter races.

Although a good student and promising athlete, Dee Dee could not come up with enough money to continue her schooling. She dropped out after her freshman year to try and earn money. The sprint coach at Cal State, Bobby Kersee, did not want to see this developing athlete lose her chance. He helped guide her through the bureaucratic maze so that she could receive financial aid and continue with her education.

Soon after, Bobby Kersee was hired away from Cal State by the University of California at Los Angeles. Dee Dee, believing that Bobby Kersee was the best coach for her, decided to follow him to UCLA.

At UCLA, Dee Dee improved very quickly, and was invited to the United States Olympic Trials in 1980. At the trials, she just missed a chance to represent the United States in the 200-meter race. And, it was her old rival, Valerie Brisco, who took her place!

This defeat encouraged Dee Dee to try even harder. She continued to train with Bobby Kersee. In 1982 she won the NCAA championship at 200 meters, with a time of 22.39 seconds. In addition to her impressive speed, Dee Dee also began to be recognized for her flamboyant style. Although most athletes were serious and solemn, Dee Dee began to impress her own style on her sport. She wanted to have fun as well as to run fast. While at UCLA, she began to grow her fingernails very long and paint and decorate them.

At the 1984 Olympic Trials, she at last earned a position as a member of the United States Olympic team. She also earned the nickname "Fluorescent Flo," for competing in bright bodysuits. In the 1984 Games, held in her home town of Los Angeles, she earned a silver medal for her time of 22.04 in the 200-meter race. She missed tying the Olympic record by just one-hundredth of a second. She was delighted by her performance, but frustrated that her old rival, Valerie Brisco, had again bested her.

Flo Jo set a record for longest fingernails on any Olympic athlete.

Griffith-Joyner celebrated after she won the 100 meters and set a new record at the 1988 Olympics.

Valerie stood on the medal stand, with a gold medal draped around her neck!

Dee Dee was also frustrated that the Soviet Union, East German, and their allies, had not sent teams to compete in these world games. In 1980, the United States had boycotted the Games in Moscow. In retaliation, many Communist countries boycotted the Los Angeles Games. Dee Dee felt incomplete: would she have medalled at all if the Soviets had been present? In addition, team officials denied Dee Dee the chance to run a leg in a sprint-relay team saying her long fingernails were a danger to the other runners. The relay teams ran, and won, without her.

Frustrated and exhausted, Dee Dee decided to stop running competitively. She stopped training hard, started a job in the employee relations department of a Los Angeles company, and gained 15 pounds.

However, Griffith was not able to forget her avocation. She began dating Al Joyner, who had

FLORENCE GRIFFITH
JOYNER: "FLO JO"

won a gold medal in the triple jump at the Los Angeles Olympics. Al's sister, Jackie Joyner-Kersee, was married to Bobby Kersee—Griffith's coach from UCLA. Almost against her will, Griffith began running competitively again in 1986.

At the World Championships, held in Rome, Florence took second in the 200 meters. Then, she ran the third leg in the first-place United States' 4 x 100 meter relay team. Next, on October 10, 1987, Al Joyner and Florence Griffith were married.

Determined to excel at the 1992 Olympics, Griffith Joyner—soon to be dubbed Flo Jo—devoted herself to her training. She returned to her old coach, Bobby Kersee. Al became her workout partner and supervisor and Florence worked out both physically and mentally. Daytime workouts were followed by late-night runs or weight-lifting sessions.

At the 1988 United States Olympic Trials, held in Indianapolis, Indiana, reporters thought Flo Jo stood a good chance or making the Olympic team again in the 200-meters. But although she had run the fastest United States times in 1985 and 1987 at 100-meters, few experts thought she was capable of upsetting world-record holder Evelyn Ashford. Bobby Kersee, however, thought differently. Ashford's world record was 10.76 for 100 meters. On a track in San Diego, running alone, Kersee had timed Florence at 10.89 for the same distance. Kersee believed the competition might give Florence the edge and added speed she needed to break the world record.

Not only was Griffith Joyner poised to set the racing world on its ear with her times, she was determined to change its staid image. While experimenting with some running tights and scissors, she had come up with a creative and interesting look. Her original costumes were wild and brightly colored. Add her brightly decorated nails, and she had the greatest presence of any runner—now she had to prove herself! As teammate Gwen Torrence said, "If you're going to wear outfits like that, then you'd better do something in them!"

On July 16th, in a qualifying meet for the 100-meter dash, Florence, dressed in a bright green, one-legged suit, raced an astonishing 10.60—well below the world record. However, when wind records were checked, it was discovered that the wind at her back was almost twice as fast as allowable.

Florence and her coach refused to be disappointed. Kersee advised Florence to check the wind speed before the beginning of her next heat. If she thought the wind had died down, she should go all out and run for the record. If the wind seemed too strong, she should relax and save herself for another heat.

In the starting blocks, Flo Jo anxiously checked the wind. It seemed to have died down somewhat, so she decided to chase the world record. She put everything she had into the heat, and was rewarded with an amazing time: 10.49—.27 seconds better than the world record! Officials assumed that her amazing time had been achieved with the help of a strong tail wind. However, when they checked the wind gauge, they were astonished to find that it registered 0.0. Griffith had smashed a world record!

In the final heat of the Trials, Flo Jo proved herself once again. Racing in an fluorescent blue-and-white suit, with fingernails painted pink, Griffith and Evelyn Ashford were placed in adjoining lanes in the track. The world watched as Florence beat Ashford by .20 seconds, a full four yards.

In her next event, the 200-meter race, she ran her first heat with the idea of breaking Valerie Brisco's United States record of 21.81. Even though she didn't run a smart race, Griffith Joyner came close with a time of 21.96. In the semifinals, she ran against her old rival, the record-holder. In a smooth, controlled heat, she reach the finish line in 21.77—a new United States record. In the final, she wore a daring all-white lace body suit and easily won the race in 21.85.

Suddenly, Olympic medals seemed within reach of the U.S. women's team. Although the formidable East Germans and Soviets would be competing in Seoul, South Korea, Florence Griffith Joyner made gold seem possible.

Flo Jo replaced her coach Bobby Kersee with her husband, Al Joyner and arrived in Seoul in 1988 confident that all her hard work was behind her. All she needed to do was remain confident and healthy. But at the air-port, Al's baggage cart tipped over, and landed on Florence's ankle!

For several days she applied ice and did nothing but stretch and pray. Fortunately, the ankle responded to the treatment and she was ready for the first heat of the 100 meters. Days earlier, she had recorded two numbers in her diary: 10.62 for the heat and 10.54 for the final.

Wearing the standard United States uniform instead of one of her fluorescent costumes, she nailed her goal for the heat: posting a 10.62 for the distance. This easily beat Ashford's old Olympic record of 10.97.

In the semifinal, Griffith Joyner was matched up with Heike Drechsler, a formidable East German coholder of the world record at this dis-tance. When she false-started at the beginning,

Sometimes it seemed Flo Jo drew more attention for her startling athletic dress than for her outstanding performances.

Florence put her race in jeopardy. Olympic sprinters are allowed only one false start. If Florence repeated her mistake, her Olympic gold medal dreams would disappear.

Determined to stay in the game, Flo Jo played it safe and got off to a slow start in the heat. By 50 meters her slow start did not matter: she passed Drechsler and pulled away from her. Griffith Joyner had run a conservative race and still beat her rival by a comfortable .21 second margin.

In her final, Flo Jo relaxed and ran her race. As former Olympic sprint champion Wilma Rudolph noted, Flo Jo walked onto the track for the finals "as if she owned it." Her gold medal time was 10.54, exactly the number she had recorded in her diary. Ashford was second with a 10.83, and Drechsler, who ran a 10.85, won the bronze.

In the 200-meters, Flo Jo ran an easy 21.56 in a qualifying heat. She seemed to run effortlessly in the finals—but her time, 21.34 seconds, set a new world record.

Finally, in the 4 x 100 relay, she ran the number three leg. Although the team's best finisher is traditionally given the fourth and final leg, Griffith Joyner gracefully returned to the number three leg she had run in Rome. Her third gold came in a team effort to win the relay.

Perhaps her only disappointment in the Games came as she anchored the 4 x 400 women's relay. Despite her best efforts, the U.S. team managed only second place. Flo Jo had three gold medals and one silver. She had the seven fastest times ever run in the women's 100 meters. She had smashed world and U.S. records with an energy and enthusiasm all her own.

Griffith Joyner's success brought with it, however, some criticism and jealousy. Near the end of the Games, Joaquim Cruz, a runner from Brazil, accused her and Jackie Joyner-Kersee of using steroids. Steroids are illegal drugs that are said to help athletes train and compete better. Cruz said, "Florence, in 1984, you could see an extremely feminine person, but today she looks more like a man than a women." Flo Jo denied any drug use and the Olympic Committee confirmed that her drug tests had been clean.

On her return to the U.S., Griffith Joyner won five prestigious awards: the C.C. Jackson Award for outstanding women track athlete of 1988; the *Associated Press* Female Athlete of the Year; she was named Athlete of the Year by the Soviet news agency, Tass; she won the 1988 Sullivan Award, which is given to the top amateur athlete in the United States; and the Jesse Owens Award for the outstanding track and field athlete of the year.

5

JACKIE JOYNER-KERSEE: THE WORLD'S GREATEST ATHLETE

Jackie Joyner was born on March 3, 1962, in East St. Louis, Illinois. Across the Missouri River from big-city St. Louis, East St. Louis is a tough and sometimes dangerous town. Jackie's parents, Alfred and Mary, had grown up there. When Mary was just 16 and Alfred just 14, Mary became pregnant with Jackie's older brother, Alfred Erick. Alfred and Mary got married and worked a variety of jobs to support their family, which grew to include Jackie and two younger sisters, Angela and Debra. The family lived in a small wooden house that had no heat; in the winters the whole family slept in the kitchen to be near the stove. Jackie's great-

---

Jackie Joyner-Kersee is the best heptathlete ever. Her strongest single event is the long jump.

grandmother, Ollie Mae Johnson, named her after Jacqueline Kennedy, wife of then-president John Kennedy. Her prediction was that baby Jackie would grow up to be "the first lady of something."

Although the Joyners had no money, Mary and Alfred were very strict with their children. Because Mary wanted a different life for her children, and her daughters especially, she made sure they were home at night "before the street lights went on," and that the girls stayed away from boys. Jackie was forbidden to date until she was eighteen. With these strict guidelines, Jackie decided to concentrate all her time and energy on her schoolwork and athletics.

Fortunately, around the corner from the Joyner home was the Mary E. Brown Community Center. Coach Nino Fennoy ran the track program at the Center. He started Jackie running the quarter-mile. She was soundly defeated in her first big meet, but the loss just made her want to train harder. Coach Finnoy remembers that "She came to practice. She had respect for adults, and discipline, and an air of enjoyment, like, 'My parents sent me here to have some fun and learn some things.' She wasn't in a hurry, she never complained." At another meet later that year she won five first-place awards. Coach Fennoy recognized, in her mental toughness and willingness to work hard, the beginnings of a world-class runner. And, at home, Jackie convinced her mother that sports might be her ticket out of East St. Louis.

A few years later, Jackie amazed Coach Fennoy by long jumping 16' 9". This would have been good jump for a high school student, but Jackie was just 12 years old! When Coach Fennoy recognized her varied abilities, he asked her if she wanted to try the pentathlon.

The pentathlon is a competition composed of five different events: the 80-meter hurdles, the 800-meter run, the long jump, the high jump, and the shot put. Jackie was delighted to try anything new and began to train in her usual diligent fashion.

In 1976, when she was 14, Jackie and her teammates earned a try at the National Junior Olympics. In that meet, Jackie won the pentathlon for her age group. Later that year, she watched Bruce Jenner's fabulous performance in the decathlon (an event made up of ten separate events) and decided to set the Olympics as her goal.

In 1977, Jackie entered Lincoln High school where she soon became an honor-roll student.

Joyner-Kersee clears a hurdle at the 1988 Olympics, where she won the gold medal in the heptathlon.

*Jackie Joyner-Kersee
gets some last minute
advice from her coach
and husband Bob
Kersee at the 1992
Olympics.*

In the fall and winter, she played volleyball and basketball. She started as forward on her basketball team as a freshman; during her last two years, the Lincoln High Tigers won the state basketball championships. College basketball coaches began to recruit her.

Springtime brought track season, and Coach Fennoy helped lead the Lincoln girls' track team to three state titles in the three years Jackie was on the team. As a junior, Jackie set the state long-jump record with a jump of 20' 7 1/2". She also won two more national junior pentathlon titles.

Jackie was not the only athlete in her family. Brother Al was also very gifted. When Jackie thought he was being lazy, she urged him to train harder. Al's best event was the triple jump. When he broke 50 feet as a high school student, he earned a college scholarship.

Both Jackie and Al were invited to the 1988 Olympic Trials. Jackie long jumped 20' 9 3/4". It was the best jump she had ever made, but that was only good enough for eighth place at the Trials.

Jackie accepted a basketball scholarship from UCLA. She decided to be a history major and was soon busy with course work and basketball practice. When she could, she also worked out with the UCLA track team. The track coaches, however, had little time for her. They devoted most of their time and energy to the athletes who were there on track scholarships. Jackie practiced her long-jumping on her own, but she only seemed to get worse, not better. However, she attracted the attention of assistant coach Bob Kersee. Coach Kersee recognized her natural ability, and began to go out of his way to help her train and practice.

In January 1981, Jackie learned her mother had been stricken with meningitis. By the time Jackie and Al got back to East St. Louis, Mary had fallen into an irreversible coma. Doctors said that she would not be able to live without life-support. Although the whole family knew that Mary would not choose to "live" like this, Alfred could not bring himself to make the decision to end his wife's life. The decision was left to Al and Jackie and, after praying together, they told the doctors to disconnect the life-support. Mary died two hours later. She was only 38 years old.

The Joyner's Aunt Della arrived to take over the running of the household. Jackie returned to UCLA, but felt as though she was deserting her family. She found comfort in Coach Kersee. He had lost his own mother when he was 18, too, and offered Jackie encouragement and support. Coach Kersee was sure that Mary would have wanted her daughter to stay in school and escape East St. Louis.

Coach Kersee knew what a great all-around athlete Jackie was, and he had a new event in mind for her: the heptathlon. This two-day competition includes four of the events of the pentathlon, adding the 200-meter run and the javelin throw and substituting the 100-meter hurdles for the 80-meter hurdles.

By late that spring, a nervous Jackie showed up at the national championships. She fell behind in the first day of competition. That night, in the hallway of their hotel, Coach Kersee marked off the long-jump runway with masking tape. They worked on her technique and the next day Jackie jumped 21 feet. It was her best jump since high school, and helped her win a third-place medal.

During her sophomore year, Jackie continued to excel on the basketball court as well as improve her hetathlon score. She was called the country's top heptathlete when she set a new college record in the event. Although she was troubled by asthma attacks, Jackie forced herself to continue. Doctors told her that if she gave up sports, she would be fine. Instead, Jackie combined a regimen of rest with medication to relieve her problem. In her junior year, Jackie was named the Most Valuable Player on both her basketball and her track teams. In June 1983 she won a second NCAA heptathlon with her record-setting 6,365 points. She also won the Broderick Award as the nation's best track college athlete.

In the summer of 1983, she and Al traveled to Finland to compete in the world track and field championships. However, both pulled hamstring muscles before competing. Al finished eighth in the triple jump and Jackie pulled out of the event without competing.

Coach Kersee convinced Jackie to sit out the 1983-1984 college basketball and track and field seasons. He wanted her to be ready and injury-free for the 1984 Olympic Trials and Games. That winter she ran in some indoor track meets. These meets gave her a chance to work on her sprinting, hurdling, and long jumping. In her daily workouts, she concentrated on her two weakest events: the shot put and javelin.

At the Olympic Trials, it was clear that her hard work had paid off. Jackie set a new American heptathlon record of 6,520 points, which included a long jump of 22' 4 1/2". Al made the Olympic team as well.

Because the U.S. had boycotted the 1980 Olympics, held in Moscow, Communist countries did not compete in the 1984 Olympics, held in Los Angeles. Jackie faced stiff competition, however, in the form of Glynis Nunn of Australia.

Jackie ended the first day of heptathlon competition in second place. On the second day, Jackie fouled on her first two long jump attempts. If she fouled again, or had a poor jump playing things safely, she'd be out of the competition. Jackie did play things safely on her third jump. She leaped a foot behind the takeoff board though still managed a jump of 20' 0 1/2". Before the final event, the 800-meter dash, Jackie had opened a very slim lead over Nunn. Jackie finished only .33 seconds behind Nunn, but Nunn's performance was enough to bring her the gold medal. Jackie missed victory by just 5 points: 6,390 to Nunn's 6,395!

Joyner-Kersee shows good form as she is about to launch the javelin at the 1992 Barcelona Olympics. She repeated as the gold-medal winner in the heptathlon.

For some athletes, a silver medal in the Olympics would have been a crowning achievement. For Jackie Joyner, it was just a starting point. She headed back to college in the fall of 1984. She performed extremely well on the basketball court, and earned a place on the All-Conference team. When the women's track season began, Coach Kersee was appointed the new head coach. With his guidance, Jackie entered sprints, hurdles, relays, and the long jump. She tried out the triple jump, too. That year, her jump of 43' 4" was the best by an American woman. At a meet in Switzerland, she sent a new American record of 23' 9". At the National Sports Festival, she won all seven heptathlon events. Her score of 6,718 points set a new college record, only 85 points shy of the U.S. record.

In the summer of 1985 Bob Kersee took her to a Houston Astros baseball game and proposed. Jackie decided to take some time off from classes to concentrate on her wedding and on track meets. She and Bob were married on January 11, 1986, in Long Beach, California. Brother Al gave Jackie away and took the wedding pictures. After a brief trip to East St. Louis, so that Bob could meet her family and see where she grew up, Jackie was back on the track—coached by her new husband.

In June, with the finish of the school year, Jackie's college sports career ended. She joined Bob's World Class Track Club. She was able to train at the club, and it entered her in meets. She won an endorsement contract from Adidas. That July, Jackie set a heptathlon record at the Goodwill Games. Then, at the U.S. Olympic Festival in Houston, she raised her own record to 7,161 points. That year she was also named recipient of the James E. Sullivan Award, given to American's best amateur athlete. In winning that award, she beat out runners-up basketball star David Robinson and football star Vinny Testaverde. In 1986, she also won the Jesse Owens Award, the Women's Athlete of the Year Award given by *Track & Field News*, and the Sportswoman of the Year Award, given by the U.S. Olympic Committee. In addition, she received her degree in history.

With the 1988 Olympics looming, Bob cut down on Jackie's work-out schedule. Plagued by aching hamstrings and a sore Achilles tendon, Jackie fought to keep training. Combined with the ever-present asthma, her injuries would have been enough to stop a lesser athlete. Jackie kept at it. She traveled and gave talks to raise money for the new Jackie Joyner-Kersee Community Foundation. Her goal was to reopen the Mary E. Brown Community Center in East St. Louis, which had been forced to close its doors in 1983.

In February, she set a U.S. indoor long-jump record of 23' 0 1/2". The next day she set another indoor record with her 60-meter high hurdles time of 7.88 seconds. Outdoors, in the 100-meter hurdles, she tied the U.S. record of 12.61 seconds. At the long-awaited Olympic Trials, Joyner-Kersee broke her own heptathlon record with 7,215 points. Then, she long jumped 24' 5" to win that event, too.

At the Olympic Games in Seoul, South Korea, Joyner-Kersee provided plenty of drama and excitement. She won the 100-meter hurdles, the first event of the heptathlon in 12.69 seconds. Then, near disaster in the high jump. Joyner-Kersee had trouble with her take-off and managed a jump of only 6' 0 1/4". At the same time, she strained a tendon in her knee. With her knee taped, she managed to put the shot 51' 10". Next, she could only manage a

22.56 second 200-meter run. That night, sports therapist Bob Forster treated her injury with ice, ultrasound, and massage.

The next day, Joyner-Kersee seemed stronger than ever. Her 23' 10 1/4" long jump brought her a new heptathlon long-jump record. Her sore knee effected her javelin performance, however, and she could only manage a throw of 149' 10". In the final event, the 800 meters, Joyner-Kersee seemed to falter in the second lap. Could she hold up? She registered a fifth-place finish with 2:08.51. Her time was quick enough to break her own world and the Olympic records: 7,291 points. Jackie had her gold medal! Five days later, in the long jump competition, she jumped 24' 3 1/2"—which gave her a new Olympic record and a second gold medal.

Joyner-Kersee's celebrations were interrupted briefly by accusations of illegal drug use by a Brazilian athlete. Jackie and her sister-in-law, Florence Griffith-Joyner, were accused of taking drugs that enhanced their performance. Both women's drug tests were clean, however, so the allegations were dismissed. Jackie was insulted. "I'm sad and sorry that people are implying that I'm doing something because I've worked hard to get where I am today."

After the Olympic Games, Joyner-Kersee's long-time rival, Cindy Greiner called her, "one of a kind." She continued, "We'll never see her likes again in track." But if she thought that the compliment might make her foe go away, she was wrong. For the next two years, Bob worked with Jackie on the hurdles. She won races at the 55-meter length. She also mastered the 400-meter hurdles, which Bob thought would help build up her endurance.

In 1990, Jackie again turned her attention to the heptathlon. She won the Goodwill Games again, seemed to lack her usual drive. A leg injury ended her season early, and an asthma attack turned into pneumonia.

A hamstring tear during the 200-meter run in the 1991 World Championships in Tokyo upset Joyner-Kersee's training. At the 1992 Olympics, held in Barcelona, Spain, Jackie traded first place back and forth with top contender Sabine Braun of Germany. On the second day, Joyner-Kersee secured her lead with a long jump of 23' 3 1/2" and then cruised through the javelin throw and 800-meter run. Sabine fell further behind. Although Joyner-Kersee suffered an asthma attack in the final 800-meter event, she had built up an insurmountable lead. Irina Belova of the Unified Team passed Braun, but still was 199 points behind Joyner-Kersee.

A few days later, Joyner-Kersee competed in the long jump competition. Her leap of 23' 2 1/2" earned her a bronze medal.

In 1992 the Women's Sports Foundation named Jackie its Amateur Sportswoman of the Year for the third time. In August 1993, Jackie won her second World Championship, again in a spirited competition with Germany's Sabine Braun.

A sore hamstring forced Jackie to withdraw from the heptathlon at the 1996 Olympic Games, held in Atlanta, Georgia. Still, the 34-year-old athlete was able to win a bronze medal in the long jump.

Joyner-Kersee has since returned to an old love—basketball. She now plays for the Richmond Rage, in an effort to help establish a new women's professional basketball league.

AFTERWORD

As women continue to set records at track and field competitions and more people come to watch the events live and on television, other athletes have become stars.

MARY DECKER SLANEY, is one of four children born to John Decker, a New Jersey tool-and-die maker and his wife, Jackie. Mary took up running formally when her family moved to Huntington Beach, California, when she was eleven. She entered a local cross-country race "on a whim" and ran to victory. By the age of 14, she had set her first world record, in the 1,000 meters. A few years later, she had the first of many surgeries. Her fierce training schedule was causing the muscles of her calves to grow too big for the sheaths surrounding them. In 1977, she went to the University of Colorado at Boulder on a full track scholarship. Although she was racing well and setting records, injuries continued to plague her. When she found that her snow-running in Boulder was causing her even more injury,

Mary Decker grimaces as she approaches the finish line of the 1983 World Track and Field championships. She overtook Zamira Zajtseva just six strides from the tape.

she moved to Eugene, Oregon, where she lives today.

Slaney is America's greatest female middle-distance runner, having racked up 36 American and 17 world records. At the 1984 Olympics she collided with Zola Budd, a South African athlete, in the final laps of the 3,000 meter race. Her tumble cost her any hopes of an Olympic medal.

She has spent recent time caring for her daughter and training with Olympic marathoner Alberto Salazar. In the fall of 1993, she set a course record of 32.38 minutes for a 10K race in Phoenix, Arizona. Slaney competed in the 1996 Atlanta Games but did not win a medal.

Gail Devers rejoices after winning the 100 meters at the 1992 Olympics.

GAIL DEVERS, a sprinter and hurdler, grew up in San Diego, California. Her father, Reverend Larry Devers, is an associate minister of the Mount Erie Baptist Church. Her mother, Alabe, worked as a teacher's aide in an elementary school. Gail describes her family life as "Leave It to Beaver," like in its simplicity and closeness. Gail started running in high school, as a distance runner. When she went to UCLA, she came under the coaching of Bobby Kersee, who saw her potential as a world-class sprinter and hurdler.

In May 1988, while a senior at UCLA, Devers set a U.S. hurdles record (12.61 seconds) and made the Olympic team in the 100-meter hurdles. Inexplicably, Gail ran poorly in Seoul. For two years she suffered vision loss, wild weight fluctuations, and fits of shaking. Finally, in 1988, doctors diagnosed her with Graves' Disease, an illness that affects the thyroid. Radiation was used to destroy a cyst and the bad part of the thyroid. However, it destroyed the entire gland! Her feet began to swell and ooze and her skin to crack and bleed. The pain was so bad that her parents had to carry her to the bathroom. Finally, the doctors changed her radiation therapy and Gail began to walk again. She had come dangerously close to having her feet amputated, though! Gail couldn't compete for two and a half years, but she came back. She won a gold medal in the 100-meter dash in the 1992 Olympic Games. In August of 1995, she won the 100-meter hurdles event for the U.S. at the World Championships. She captured the gold in this event as well at the 1996 Olympics.

TEGLA LOROUPE is a small (5' 0 1/4") and quiet marathoner who captured the New York City Marathon in 1994 and 1995. A postal auditor at home in Kenya, her victory in 1994 made her the first black woman to win a major marathon. At 21, she was also one of the youngest women ever to win the New York City marathon. She became a feminist symbol when she noted that Kenya, noted for its male runners, discourages women from running. Her victory means that Kenyan sports officials will have to offer her a place on their country's Olympic team. Although she was too shy to tell the New York Road Runners Club that they had been misspelling her name for two years, she took home $20,000 in prize money and a brand new Mercedes Benz. Still in top form, she won the 1995 race just days after the death of her beloved sister.

Since 1972, when Congress passed Title IX, a law that created new opportunities for female athletes, women have had a chance to compete in more and ever tougher venues. With determination, dedication, and lots of hard work these women have inspired us all. They are truly champions.

SUGGESTONS FOR FURTHER READING

Cohen, Neil. *Jackie Joyner-Kersee*. Boston: Little, Brown & Company, 1992.

Green, Carl R. *Jackie Joyner-Kersee*. New York: Crestwood House, Macmillan Publishing Company, 1994.

Laklan, Carli. *Golden Girls: True Stories of Olympic Women* Stars. New York: McGraw-Hill, 1980.

Myers, Gail Anderson. *A World of Sports for Girls*. Philadelphia: The Westminster Press, 1981.

Siegel, Alice and McLoone, Margo. *It's a Girl's Game Too*. New York: Holt, Rinehart and Winston, 1980.

Waitz, Grete and Averbuch, Gloria. *World Class*. New York: Warner Books, 1986.

ABOUT THE AUTHOR

MARTHA WICKHAM works for a large publishing company as an editor of children's books. She has written over ten books for children and currently lives in Queens, New York.

INDEX

Picture Credits

AP/Wide World: pp. 2, 8, 11, 16, 21, 29, 32, 35, 42, 55; Corbis: pp. 14, 24, 38, 41, 46, 48, 51, 52, 60, 61.